WHY WAR HAPPENED

WHAT CAUSED THE
AFGHANISTAN
WAR?

BY SARAH LEVETE

Gareth Stevens
PUBLISHING

Please visit our website, www.garethstevens.com.
For a free color catalog of all our high-quality books,
call toll free 1-800-542-2595 or fax 1-877-542-2596.

Cataloging-in-Publication Data

Names: Levete, Sarah.
Title: What caused the Afghanistan War? / Sarah Levete.
Description: New York : Gareth Stevens Publishing, 2017. | Series: Why war happened | Includes index.
Identifiers: ISBN 9781482451849 (pbk.) | ISBN 9781482451788 (library bound) | ISBN 9781482451689 (6 pack)
Subjects: LCSH: Afghan War, 2001--Juvenile literature.
Classification: LCC DS371.412 L48 2017 | DDC 958.104'7--dc23

First Edition

Published in 2017 by
Gareth Stevens Publishing
111 East 14th Street, Suite 349
New York, NY 10003

© 2017 Gareth Stevens Publishing

Produced by Calcium
Editors: Sarah Eason and Harriet McGregor
Designer: Jessica Moon
Picture researcher: Harriet McGregor

Picture credits: Cover: Getty: JANGIR/AFP (photo), Shutterstock: kasha_malasha (bkgrd). Insides: Shutterstock: Alenvl 11, Nate Derrick 33, 43, 45, Karen Faljyan 26, Gaborbasch 21, Khlongwangchao 7, Morphart Creation 15, Northfoto 23, Lizette Potgieter 5, Skyearth 13, Ken Tannenbaum 25, Pal Teravagimov 22, Przemek Tokar 35, Dana Ward 9; Wikimedia Commons: Sgt. 1st Class Jim Downen/U.S. Army 41, Erwin Franzen 29, Colonel Gentil 14, Кувакнн E. (1985) 18, Karla Marshall/U.S. Army Corps of Engineers 27, Master Sgt. Michael O'Connor/U.S. Air Force 17, U.S. Navy 31, Daniel Wilkinson/U.S. Department of State 39, Edgar Zessinthal 37.

Printed in the United States of America
CPSIA compliance information: Batch #CS16GS: For further information contact Gareth Stevens, New York, New York at 1-800-542-2595.

CONTENTS

Words in the glossary appear in **bold** type
the first time they are used in the text.

CHAPTER I

ABOUT AFGHANISTAN

Many people in Afghanistan have only known their country to be involved in war and conflict. They have been born into a country that is exhausted by wars. Their grandparents and great-grandparents lived in a country plagued by either Afghan people fighting one another, or troops from other countries.

In this book, we look at the Afghanistan War that started in 2001. At the time of writing, there are still foreign troops in the country, and **civilians** continue to be targeted by the extremist groups that the war was intended to destroy.

We explore the background and buildup to the war in Afghanistan. We look at the **political** views that influenced the war and explore how the country's history influenced events that led to war. We examine the effect of the war and reflect on how the war's outcome affected the countries involved. There were many factors that led to the Afghanistan War. It is important to question whether war was inevitable or whether at any stage it could have been avoided or shortened.

SUFFERING

Thousands of **military** men and women from many countries lost their lives in the Afghanistan War. Innocent civilians have become caught up in it. The question is now, how can peace happen in Afghanistan?

Afghan children have lived with years of conflict and fighting.
These children in Kabul are burning trash to warm their hands.

In any war, opposing sides have different views on why a war starts and their reasons for sending men and women to fight. There is often no single reason for the start of a war. Understanding the reasons behind a country's decision to send its men and women to fight cannot undo the tragedy of lives lost or the disaster experienced by those caught up in the conflict. It can, however, help prevent further conflict or at least make people aware of the consequences of going to war.

THE COUNTRY

Afghanistan is a country of mountains, deserts, and deep valleys. Winters are harsh and cold, with heavy snowfall. Summers are dry and hot. Afghanistan experiences severe natural disasters such as earthquakes and droughts. Travel through Afghanistan is often difficult, due to the treacherous landscape. Foreign forces have struggled to **dominate** in the country's remote and isolated areas.

The country has an area of 250,000 sq miles (647,500 sq km), which is a little smaller than the state of Texas. It borders lie next to Pakistan, Iran, Turkmenistan, Uzbekistan, Tajikistan, and China. Afghanistan's key location between the Middle East and South and Central Asia has made it important to other nations. This partly accounts for why it has had so many foreign invasions. Although they have been attracted by Afghanistan's location, invaders have found it difficult to cope with the challenges presented by its unforgiving landscape and harsh winter climate.

Afghanistan is a farming country and has a wealth of natural resources such as natural gas. However, years of conflict and a lack of money have not allowed Afghanistan to mine these resources and take advantage of them.

HINDU KUSH

The towering Hindu Kush chain of mountains runs northeast to southwest across the country, dividing the northern areas of Afghanistan from the other parts. One of the world's highest mountain ranges, it forms part of the boundary between eastern Afghanistan and northwestern Pakistan. Within these huge mountains, there are deep fertile valleys, narrow mountain passes, and dry deserts.

The Hindu Kush mountain range is 500 miles (800 km) long and 150 miles (240 km) wide.

The Khyber Pass cuts through the mountains that divide Pakistan and Afghanistan. It has been an incredibly important route between Afghanistan and Pakistan and has been used by invading forces to enter Afghanistan. During the recent Afghanistan War, the United States and the **North Atlantic Treaty Organization (NATO)** forces used the pass to bring arms and troops into the country. NATO is an organization that defends countries in need. Afghans have used it as an escape route to leave the country and find refuge in neighboring Pakistan.

THE PEOPLE

Generations of Afghan people have experienced conflict and war. The country has been invaded by foreign powers seeking to impose their rule upon the country. The Afghan people have continued to put up fierce resistance and fight for their independence. The country has also experienced terrible fighting between groups of Afghan people.

The name "Afghanistan" means "Land of the Afghans." The Afghan people come from many different tribes, or traditional communities, and **ethnic** groups. The largest ethnic group is the Pashtuns, or Durrani people. Other groups include the Tajiks, Hazaras, Uzbeks, Turkmans, Aimaqa, and Nuristanis. Many languages are spoken in Afghanistan, reflecting the range of different ethnic groups. Afghan Persian is spoken by about half of the population. Pashtu is spoken by around one-third.

For centuries, parts of Afghanistan society have been organized around tribal groups. Tribal elders lead these distinct local groups, responsible for **justice** and organizing their community. Tribes are often isolated in remote areas and high mountains. During the Soviet invasion (see pages 18–19), different tribes united against the invaders. When the Soviets left the country, the tribes began to battle each other for power. During the recent Afghanistan War, opposing sides wanted to gain support from the influential tribal leaders.

Afghanistan is a very poor country, with little education available for the majority of people. The country also has one of the lowest rates of literacy in the world. Two-thirds of the population cannot read or write.

Religious beliefs are key to the structure of society in Afghanistan.

RELIGION

Islamic religion lies at the root of Afghan society, affecting almost every aspect of people's lives, from how they dress to how they educate their children. An estimated 80 percent of the population follows the Sunni branch of Islam; the rest follow Shi'a Islam. A tiny proportion of the population follows other religions including Hinduism and Sikhism.

CHAPTER 2

INVASION HISTORY

Afghanistan was once home to some of the earliest-known farming communities. Many different tribes of people lived there, and the land was divided into different areas or provinces.

Several rulers from other lands tried to conquer the land we now know as Afghanistan, and for centuries the country was part of different **empires**. In 330 BC, Greek Alexander the Great (356–323 BC) led his army across the Hindu Kush, enduring terrible conditions and hunger. Alexander managed to gain control of most of the land. But, when he left to extend his empire in nearby India in 327 BC, fighting broke out in different provinces. Following Alexander's death, the country was split up again, ruled by different groups who fought for control over their regions for hundreds of years.

During the seventh century AD, Muslim Arabs arrived in Afghanistan and Islam was introduced to the country. In 1221, the Mongols invaded Afghanistan. Led by Genghis Khan (1162–1227), the Mongols were ruthless invaders, but the native people of the land put up huge resistance, just as they would to the Soviets centuries later. Mongolian conquerors controlled much of the region until the sixteenth century, although they continued to face opposition to their rule. When the Mongol rule collapsed, the Mughals from northern India and the Safavids from Iran fought over the land. Afghanistan was devastated by the years of bitter fighting over its land.

Genghis Khan and his Mongol army conquered huge chunks of Asia and China. Khan created the largest land empire in history. It was the size of Africa.

DIFFERENT INFLUENCES

Buddhist temples were built during the sixth century, reflecting the early influence of the Buddhist religion in Afghanistan. About 1,400 years later, the temples were destroyed by an extremist group, the Taliban, who wanted to destroy any non-Islamic sites in the country.

A HISTORY OF WAR

The background to the Afghanistan War began centuries ago. Afghanistan has been affected by foreign invasions and influences for hundreds of years, and has been ripped apart by internal conflict.

A summary of the events that led to the war in 2001:

330 BC Alexander the Great invades modern day Afghanistan.

1220 Genghis Khan and other Mongol armies arrive in Afghanistan.

1747 Ahmad Shah Durrani (1722–1772), an Afghan tribal leader, takes control.

1826 Dost Mohammad (1793–1863) takes the throne in Afghanistan.

1839 The First Anglo-Afghan War starts.

1840 Dost Mohammad surrenders to the British.

1842 The First Anglo-Afghan War ends.

1843 Dost Mohammad is restored to the throne.

1878 The Second Anglo-Afghan War starts.

1880 The Second Anglo-Afghan War ends.

1919–1929 Amanullah Khan (1892–1960) rules the newly recognized kingdom of Afghanistan.

1933–1973 Mohammed Zahir Shah (1914–2007) is king.

1973 Mohammed Daud Khan (1909–1978) takes over as ruler.

1978 Mohammed Daud Khan is overthrown.

1979 The **Soviet Union** sends in troops.

1989 The last Soviet troops leave.

12

Foreign invaders have struggled with the challenges of Afghanistan's treacherous landscape.

13

EMPIRE BUILDING

In 1747, Ahmad Shah Durrani, a Pashtun Afghan tribal leader, took control of most of what is now Afghanistan. Ahmad united different Afghan tribes, but following his death there was chaos and conflict between the tribal groups. In the early nineteenth century, Afghanistan became caught between two new enemies, Britain and Russia.

Britain and Russia were busy building their empires during the eighteenth and nineteenth centuries. Britain had already laid claim to several other countries, including the West Indies and India. Russia wanted to develop a trading link with Asia. In order to do this, it would need the support of a government in Afghanistan. The country was becoming a political football played between two powerful countries.

Ahmad Shah Durrani not only controlled Afghanistan, he also invaded India nine times.

Britain and Russia were suspicious of each other's intentions in Afghanistan, as each side tried to outsmart the other. This became known as "The Great Game." It had a terrible effect on Afghanistan. The British were worried that Russia would use Afghanistan to help them invade India, and threaten British domination there. The British did not want the leader of Afghanistan, Dost Mohammad, to have any contact with the Russians. Although Dost Mohammad tried to maintain peace between the two countries, the British invaded, seizing major cities in Afghanistan. This was the First Anglo-Afghan War. In 1842, the British suffered a massive defeat. However, within 40 years, once again the British used force against the people of Afghanistan.

BRITISH DEFEAT

In January 1842, in bitter, icy conditions, local Afghan tribesmen overwhelmed the British. The British suffered the loss of thousands of men. There was one survivor from the British Army, Dr. William Brydon (1811–1873), who later said,

"This was a terrible march, the fire of the enemy incessant, and numbers of officers and men, not knowing where they were going from snow-blindness, were cut up."

This illustration shows the return of the lone survivor, Dr. Brydon.

FIGHTING FOR INDEPENDENCE

Despite their withdrawal, the British were still determined to have a hold in Afghanistan, and to prevent the Russians laying claim to the country. The British were furious when a Russian official was granted permission to enter the country, yet a British official had not been granted permission. In 1878, the British sent troops into the country, beginning the Second Anglo-Afghan War. Although the British governed the country, they did not have the support of the people and ruthlessly stifled ongoing resistance. Afghanistan resistance did not dwindle. In 1880, the British withdrew.

In 1907, the Russians and British signed an agreement, dividing up their interests in both Iran and Afghanistan. A treaty, in 1919, declared that Afghanistan was "free and independent in its internal and external affairs." In 1919, Afghanistan was independent, but for how long?

Amanullah Khan led Afghanistan when it gained independence from Britain. He tried to bring more modern ideas to Afghanistan, such as not making it compulsory for women to wear a veil and introducing schools that took both boys and girls. These ideas were not popular with the traditional views of many tribal leaders. When Amanullah was forced to step down, Afghanistan was thrown again into turmoil as different groups in the country fought for power. In 1933, Mohammed Zahir Shah (1914–2007) took to the throne. He would rule for the next 40 years.

Afghan people celebrate Independence Day on August 19 to commemorate signing the treaty of independence in 1919.

NEW PARTNERS

In 1917, the Afghans agreed a treaty of friendship with the new communist government in the Soviet Union. This friendship ended disastrously when the Soviet Union invaded the country in 1979.

CHAPTER 3

THE SOVIET EFFECT

After World War II, the United States and the Soviet Union emerged as powerful nations. They held opposite views about politics and the way countries should be governed, and were wary of one another's power. Neither the United States nor the Soviet Union wanted to go to war with each other because it would have led to another catastrophic world war. Instead, they fought each other in different ways. They began what is known as the Cold War. Instead of a direct war, the superpowers fought for power by trying to gain control of other countries, including Afghanistan.

Many Afghans were taken prisoner by the invading Soviets.

DURING THE SOVIET INVASION

More than 1 million people died (mainly civilians) and 1.5 million were made disabled.
2 million people had to leave their homes.
5 million **refugees** fled to Pakistan and Iran.
Thousands of villages were destroyed.
13,000 Soviet troops were killed.
The Soviet Union collapsed a few years later after it withdrew from Afghanistan.

For more than 40 years, Afghanistan experienced a period of some stability under Mohammed Zahir Shah. He introduced a number of reforms, including more freedom for women. The country received huge amounts of **aid** from both the Soviet Union and the United States. He and his government developed **economic** links to the Soviet Union. Thousands of Afghans joined the military and were trained in the Soviet Union.

In 1973, Zahir Shah stood down. His departure was followed by many changes in leadership. On April 27, 1978, a Soviet-supported **communist** government took control of the country, but tribal groups rebelled against the government's more modern ideas, such as giving men and women equal rights. In September 1979, Afghan leader Hafizullah Amin (1929–1979) took control of the communist government for a short time. The Soviets were worried that he was developing links with the United States. They decided to intervene and put in place their own leader, Babrak Kamal (1929–1996). Amin was killed during the unrest.

In 1979, the Soviet Union sent troops to support Kamal's government. This started a nine-year campaign that cost countless lives and severely damaged Afghanistan. It was a shockingly violent war that devastated the country and people. By its end, it had created the unsettled environment and fighting groups that were to play a critical role in the 2001 Afghanistan War.

RESISTANCE GROUPS

From 1979, despite their large number of troops and weapons, the Soviets were unable to defeat the growing unrest and rebellion amongst the Afghan people. Groups of resistance fighters, known as the mujahideen, called for a holy war to defeat the Soviet troops, who were not Muslim. The Americans did not want the Soviets to extend communist power, so the United States and their ally and Afghanistan's neighbor, Pakistan, gave the mujahideen financial support and weapons. The Cold War was heating up. Afghanistan was becoming a battleground.

The Soviet Union took control of the main cities, but was unable to remove its control into more rural and isolated areas. Many Arabs joined the call to expel the Soviets, including a wealthy Saudi Arabian man named Osama bin Laden (1957–2011). He was to play a key role in the following conflict.

After nine years of fierce and bloody fighting, the Soviet Union withdrew its forces in 1989. As the Soviets withdrew from Afghanistan, a powerful new group was emerging. The Taliban began as a group of religious students, many of whom were educated in **madrassas** in northern Pakistan, where they had fled after the Soviet invasion. The madrassas taught students extremist views.

EXTREMIST VIEWS

The Taliban have extremist Islamic views. These are not the views of moderate Muslims. The Taliban forbids girls over the age of eight from attending school, bans television, music, and movie theaters, and requires women to wear a full covering veil, called a burka, in public. Women are only allowed out if accompanied by a male relative. Punishments for breaking Taliban laws are brutal, and include cutting off limbs and executions.

During the Soviet invasion, millions of Afghans, such as this man, became refugees, and fled to neighboring countries including Pakistan. Since the recent Afghanistan War, many more Afghans have sought refuge in other countries.

CIVIL WAR

The Soviet troops had left, but the Soviet-backed president remained. The country was thrown into even more chaos. Aid from the United States decreased now that, following the Soviets' departure, they no longer considered Afghanistan important. The country had been ruined by the Soviet invasion, and now it was to be further destroyed by **civil war**.

In 1992, different groups of mujahideen came together to overthrow the Soviet-backed president. Burhanuddin Rabbani (1940–2011) led a new government, but the different groups began fighting one another. Once again, Afghanistan was a country made of areas ruled by rival tribal leaders. The civil war lasted for four years.

The Taliban took advantage of the chaos in the country. They promised law, order, and stability. By 1998, the Taliban controlled about 90 percent of the country. However, Taliban rule was ruthless and cruel, particularly for women. On Friday

This young boy would not have been allowed to fly a kite under Taliban rule.

This soldier fought on the side of an Afghan leader against the Taliban during the mid-1990s.

THE NORTHERN ALLIANCE

The Northern Alliance came together to resist the advance of the Taliban. It is made up of different ethnic groups of rebels, many of whom had fought each other before the Taliban gained control. The Northern Alliance held control of the northeast of Afghanistan. Burhanuddin Rabbani was one of its senior leaders. In September 2001, a senior member of the Northern Alliance was killed in a suicide bombing, thought to have been carried out by al-Qaeda, a **terrorist** organization with close ties to the Taliban. This was days before the attack on the United States that triggered the Afghanistan War.

nights, the sports stadium was not open for sporting events. Instead, people were publicly executed there. The popular activity of kite-flying was banned. Non-Muslim cultural sites, including the Buddha statues in Bamiyan, were destroyed. Only three countries, Pakistan, Saudi Arabia, and the United Arab Emirates, recognized the Taliban as Afghanistan's legitimate government.

CHAPTER 4

9/11 AND BEYOND

After the Soviet invasion, there followed years of chaos. Then, major terrorist attacks in the United States propelled Afghanistan into another war that was to last for more than a decade, further ravaging the country.

On September 11, 2001, on a crisp fall morning, people in New York City and Washington, D.C., were going about their daily routines. Terrorists hijacked four airplanes full of passengers. They flew two of the planes deliberately and directly into the two towers of the World Trade Center in New York City. The towers were destroyed when the planes crashed into them. On the same morning, a third plane hit the Pentagon just outside Washington, D.C., and the fourth plane crashed in a field in Pennsylvania. More than 3,000 people died.

The United States identified Osama bin Laden and al-Qaeda as the agents behind the terrorist attacks. They believed that the terrorists had been trained and hidden in Afghanistan. The Taliban refused to reveal the whereabouts of bin Laden.

On October 7, 2001, the United States began Operation Enduring Freedom, also known as the War on Terror. This was an American-led international effort to end the Taliban regime in Afghanistan and destroy Osama bin Laden's terrorist network there.

HUNTING THE TERRORISTS

On the evening of 9/11, President George W. Bush (born 1946) broadcast a press statement on television. He declared:

"We will make no distinction between the terrorists who committed these acts and those who harbor them."

Smoke pours from the top of one of the towers after it was hit by a hijacked plan in the 9/11 attacks. Minutes later, the entire tower crumbled to the ground.

TERRORIST GROUPS

When the Taliban took power, it was led by Mullah Omar (c. 1960–2013). He had worked alongside Osama bin Laden during the Soviet invasion. Mullah Omar allowed al-Qaeda to stay in Afghanistan. It was this decision, and the decision not to reveal the whereabouts of bin Laden, that led to the latest war in Afghanistan. The United States was convinced that bin Laden was the brains behind the terrible events of 9/11. Omar refused the United States' demands to give up bin Laden.

Osama bin Laden was the son of wealthy parents. When the Soviets invaded Afghanistan, bin Laden traveled to Pakistan to meet Afghan rebel leaders. He then returned to Saudi Arabia to gather weapons and money to fund the mujahideen groups, and to join them. When the Soviets withdrew, bin Laden returned to his native country, but he was angered when the Saudi Arabians

Osama bin Laden founded the terrorist organization, al-Qaeda, held responsible for the attacks of 9/11.

Terrorist group al-Qaeda ran training camps in Afghanistan, training extremists in the use of weapons and terrorist tactics.

WHAT IS TERRORISM?

Terrorism is the use of violence to achieve political gains. Terrorists are not interested in **democracy** or trying to persuade people of their views through debate. They want to bring about change through violence and terror, making people so frightened that they will accept their views.

welcomed U.S. soldiers into the country. He was forced to leave Saudi Arabia and went to Sudan for five years. During this time, his following was increasing. He called for a war on the United States, and on Jews, and he wanted to free Islamic holy sites from any non-Muslims.

The Taliban wanted to govern Afghanistan according to extremist interpretations of Islam. Al-Qaeda also adopts extremist views, but it wants to impose its extremist beliefs in as many countries as possible. It is an international terrorist organization.

BORDERS

Afghanistan has approximately 3,500 miles (5,630 km) of border. Borders can create tensions with neighboring countries. In 1893, the British had "drawn" a border between British India and Afghanistan. This became known as the Durand Line, after the man who drew the line, Sir Mortimer Durand (1850–1924). The boundary divided the land that mainly belonged to the Pashtun people.

In 1947, India had gained independence from the British. This led to the creation of a new nation, Pakistan. India was split into Muslim Pakistan and Hindu India. As soon as this happened, Afghanistan requested changes to the Durand Line, which was a legacy of British intervention in India. Afghanistan called for a new state called "Pashtunistan." This would mean that the Pashtun people would no longer be divided between Pakistan and Afghanistan. Pakistan refused.

Pakistan had supported the United States during the Cold War. They felt threatened by the Soviet invasion of Afghanistan. Alongside the United States, Pakistan supported the Afghan rebels (mujahideen) against the Soviets, and this helped the Taliban grow. Pakistan was also one of only three countries, along with Saudi Arabia and the United Arab Emirates, that recognized the Taliban when they were in power in Afghanistan from the mid-1990s until 2001. After the events of 9/11, Pakistan supported the United States' War on Terror.

The Pakistan Taliban rules an area of northern Pakistan along uncontrolled border areas. In 2012, the group was responsible for the attempt to kill teenager Malala Yousafzai (born 1997). She had spoken up for the right of girls to go to school.

This photograph shows mujahideen crossing over the Durand line from Pakistan into Afghanistan.

MADRASSAS IN PAKISTAN

Many of Taliban's leaders are believed to have been educated in Pakistan, in refugee camps where they had fled with millions of other Afghans after the Soviet invasion. Pakistan provided education and support for refugees in many of these camps.

OPERATION ENDURING FREEDOM

The aim of Operation Enduring Freedom was to find Osama bin Laden, remove the Taliban from power, and prevent terrorists using Afghanistan as a base and hideout. The attack on Afghanistan began in 2001. It would be another 14 years before the last foreign fighting troops would leave the country.

In November 2001, B-1 and B-52 bombers began to strike suspected al-Qaeda targets at night. The Taliban government, based in the capital city, Kabul, fell in December 2001. The Taliban fled, moving toward the border with Pakistan.

Mullah Omar and Osama bin Laden were two of the most wanted men in the world. In early December 2001, Afghan troops fought fierce battles near the Tora Bora caves, where Taliban leaders Mullah Omar and Osama Bin Laden were believed to be hiding. After a two-week battle and many hundreds of deaths, it became clear that both suspects had escaped.

In December 2001, world leaders and Afghan politicians met in the German city, Bonn, to find a way for Afghanistan to find stability and peace. The Taliban were

DEATH OF OSAMA BIN LADEN

Some people wanted Osama bin Laden to face justice and be tried for his crimes. However, after years of searching, an American operation on May 2, 2011, led to the death of the al-Qaeda leader. He was discovered hiding in a large house in Pakistan. Special Forces troops attacked in the dead of night. Bin Laden was killed.

An American fighter pilot controls his aircraft
in a combat mission over Afghanistan.

not invited to the meeting. Plans were made to hold elections in Afghanistan.
These were held in 2004, and Hamid Karzai (born 1957) was elected president.
Peace however, was a long way off. The Taliban renewed their campaign against
American and other troops in Afghanistan. At the time of writing, the Taliban
are still engaged in a violent conflict to impose their rule on the country.

 In 2004 and 2005, there were elections to vote for a president and
parliament. About 40 percent of women voted. A fixed number of seats in the
government were reserved for women. This was significant progress in such
a male-dominated country.

CHAPTER 5

THE LONG WAR

The Afghanistan War involved men and women from more than 40 countries. The Afghan Northern Alliance, the Afghan Army, and other international forces worked together alongside the United States. From 2003, NATO led the International Security Assistance Forces (ISAF), which was a security mission in Afghanistan.

In 2002, President Karzai had announced the creation of a new Afghan National Army (ANA). Before this, law and order was governed by groups of armed men under the command of warlords. The ANA worked with international troops, making up the ISAF. The majority of troops came from the United States and Britain.

From 2011, the United States and its **allies** decided to reduce the number of troops in Afghanistan, and the ANA took on responsibility for preventing the return of the Taliban and keeping security in the country. This has yet to be fully successful.

The United States attacked Afghanistan to defeat the Taliban, destroy al-Qaeda's safe haven, and make the world a safer place. Within two months of attacking, the Taliban had been removed from power. However, 13 years later, the United States were still a force in Afghanistan, with troops defending themselves against the Taliban, which continued to launch attacks. The United States and NATO formally ended their combat role in Afghanistan in 2014. Troops remain in Afghanistan to support the Afghan forces, help rebuild the shattered country, and prevent a return of Taliban rule.

In 2015, ISAF began a smaller noncombat mission called "Resolute Support." This aims to train, advise, and support the Afghan security forces and institutions.

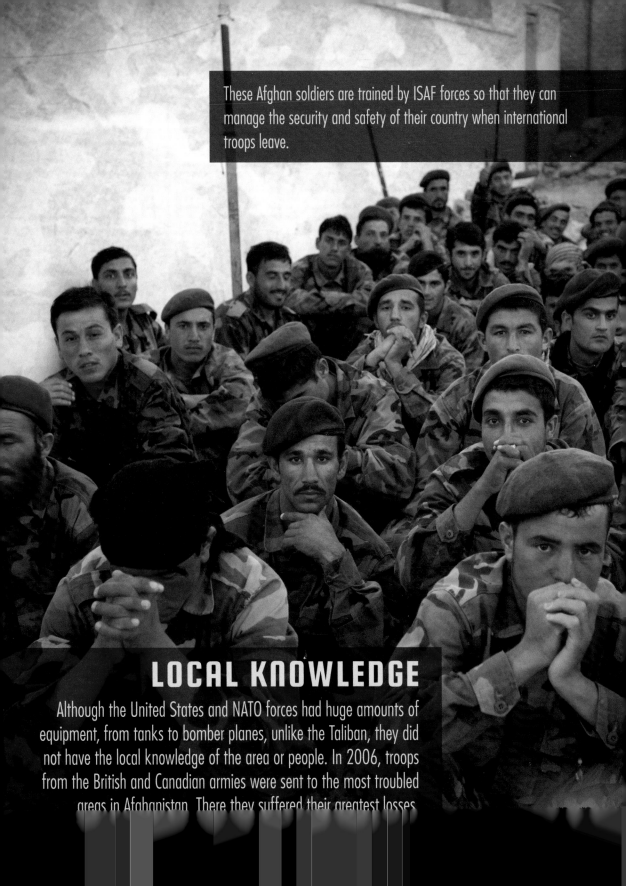

These Afghan soldiers are trained by ISAF forces so that they can manage the security and safety of their country when international troops leave.

LOCAL KNOWLEDGE

Although the United States and NATO forces had huge amounts of equipment, from tanks to bomber planes, unlike the Taliban, they did not have the local knowledge of the area or people. In 2006, troops from the British and Canadian armies were sent to the most troubled areas in Afghanistan. There they suffered their greatest losses.

CHANGE OF DIRECTION

The Afghanistan War was one of the longest wars that the United States has been involved in. The U.S. military was supported by NATO troops. However, they could not swiftly unite the country. The war began to get rid of the Taliban and al-Qaeda. Once the Taliban appeared to have gone, it became about rebuilding the country.

At first, many Afghans welcomed ISAF forces. They offered a hope of security and safety for those who had long suffered under the brutal Taliban regime. ISAF forces needed the support of ordinary Afghans to help them prevent a return of Taliban rule. However, as the war continued, many Afghans became impatient with the slow pace of progress in their country's development. They became angered by the corruption of local leaders and the government. Such views made it much easier for the Taliban to infiltrate communities. By the beginning of 2005, the Taliban were regrouping and were back on the attack. International troops were trying to protect the civilians from the Taliban. Many Afghans despaired. Why was the Taliban able to return?

UNITED STATES' INTENTION

In April 2002, President Bush declared the United States' intention in Afghanistan:

"... we expect ... trained killers to try to regroup, to murder, create mayhem, and try to undermine Afghanistan's efforts to build a lasting peace ... We know this from not only intelligence, but from the history of military conflict in Afghanistan. It's been one of initial success, followed by long years of floundering and ultimate failure. We're not going to repeat that mistake.'" "Peace will be achieved by helping Afghanistan develop its own stable government. Peace will be achieved by helping Afghanistan train and develop its own national army. And peace will be achieved through an education system for boys and girls which works."

Thousands of civilians were caught up in the conflict. Sometimes, rockets fired by the international troops hit the wrong target, killing innocent Afghans. The Taliban lined up women and children on a roof and then fired at enemy troops from behind this "human shield." If the troops did not react, they would die. If they did react, they risked killing innocent people. The Taliban knew how damaging it was for ISAF when they mistakenly killed civilians.

Some viewed the foreign troops as invaders of their country; others viewed them as liberators, who would free the country from the brutal rule of the Taliban.

REACTING TO WAR

At the start of the war, public opinion in the United States was generally in favor of the use of troops to remove the Taliban and al-Qaeda groups. However, as the war continued, and more and more troops were injured or lost their lives, public opinion changed.

The war had become about rebuilding Afghanistan, but the troops were still at risk. The public could not see an end to the casualties or significant change in Afghanistan. Polls in both the United States and Britain (countries providing the largest number of troops) showed a decline in public opinion for the support of the war.

The Afghanistan War became very unpopular with the American public. Many could not understand why their troops were suffering in a country far away, trying to rebuild another country. This was at a time when the United States was also at war in Iraq. In neither conflict has there been a clear resolution. Each country is still plagued by violence and uncertainty. Extremist groups take advantage of this instability. It makes it easier for them to attract support from ordinary people who are exhausted by conflict and failure in their country.

THE IRAQ WAR

On March 20, 2003, President Bush ordered the invasion of Iraq. The Americans believed that the Iraqis held "Weapons of Mass Destruction," such as nuclear and chemical weapons. Some countries, including Britain and Australia, supported the attack. However, many members of the United Nations, including France and Germany, did not. The war lasted for eight years. An extremist Islamic group that calls itself the Islamic State of Iraq and Syria (ISIS) began to gain hold in some areas. This organization continues to carry out some of the worst terrorist atrocities around the world.

Protesters in the United States and allied countries voiced their anger at U.S. involvement in the Afghanistan War.

The Taliban and al-Qaeda hold extremist views about the Islamic religion and want to impose those views on everyone. They use force and violence to achieve this. Other groups with similar aims have developed around the world, carrying out devastating terrorist atrocities. In Paris in 2015, gunmen belonging to an extremist group, the so-called ISIS, shot dead more than 30 people in one evening. The group is believed to be active in Afghanistan. Even by the Taliban's strict and brutal rule, the acts of violence carried out by ISIS are shocking. There are fears that the group is trying to take over from the Taliban in Afghanistan.

AT WAR

After the 9/11 attacks on the United States, American and British troops responded by launching attacks on Afghanistan. International troops are still involved in peace keeping and rebuilding the devastated country, 15 years after the Americans first targeted al-Qaeda.

The key events of the war:

2001

September 11 Al-Qaeda hijack four American planes, crashing two into the World Trade Center, one into the Pentagon, and one comes down in a field. More than 3,000 people die.

October 7 American and British forces bomb Taliban strongholds and troops are sent to Afghanistan.

November 13 The Northern Alliance take control of the Afghan capital Kabul.

December 20 The U.N. Security Council establishes the ISAF.

December 9 The Taliban surrender the city of Kandahar.

2002

NATO allies and U.S. troops work with the Northern Alliance to protect Afghanistan from the Taliban.

2003

May 1 The United States declares that combat in Afghanistan is over.

2004

October 9 Afghans vote in the first election for 35 years. Karzai is elected as the leader of Afghanistan.

2014

December NATO hands authority over to Afghan forces, but 2014 is the bloodiest year in Afghanistan since 2001.

2015

January The NATO-led mission "Resolute Support" begins. Members of the mission continue to train and support Afghan security forces.

The Afghan Border Police have a challenging task patrolling the country's borders, to prevent terrorists entering the country and to prevent drug-smuggling.

CHAPTER 6

THE LEGACY AND LESSONS

The Afghanistan War has had no definitive end or result. American troops are still in the country, supporting the ANA and running operations against the Taliban. President Barack Obama (born 1961) aims to end U.S. military involvement in the country in 2017. There have been advances for the country, and there have been setbacks. No one yet knows what the future holds for Afghanistan.

At the end of 2014, 90 percent of U.S. troops had been withdrawn from Afghanistan. President Obama acknowledged that American troops and military intelligence had successfully destroyed the terrorist cells or groups responsible for 9/11, and disrupted many terrorist plots. However, he went on to say,

> "Afghanistan remains a dangerous place . . . The United States . . . will maintain a limited military presence in Afghanistan to train, advise, and assist Afghan forces and to conduct counterterrorism operations."

On September 28, 2015, the Taliban took control of Kunduz, a northern Afghanistan city. The following day Afghan forces supported by U.S. air strikes retook Kunduz. One air strike hit a hospital run by Doctors Without Borders, a worldwide medical agency, killing 22 people, including 12 hospital staff members and 7 patients, and badly damaging the hospital. Within days, Doctors Without Borders left Kunduz. Afghanistan is not yet at peace.

CONTINUING CONFLICT

One major advance in the country is the availability of education for both girls and boys. In 2001, no girls attended formal schools and there were only 1 million boys enrolled. According to the World Bank, 7.8 million pupils now attend school, and about 2.9 million of those pupils are girls. More women are now able to read and write, skills that will enable them to work and to help provide for their families.

The long-term effects of military action in Afghanistan are not yet known.

THE PRICE OF WAR

No one can put a figure on the damage caused by the Afghanistan War. The soldiers who have been killed or wounded, the civilians who have lived in terror and danger—each one of those affected, and their families, will suffer the experience of war for the rest of their lives.

Before the most recent war, Afghanistan was already in turmoil because of poverty, particularly in very rural and isolated parts of the country. Earthquakes often rock the country, killing people and destroying homes and buildings. Years of unrest had destroyed proper organization within the government. There were few effective ways to provide essentials such as clean water, healthcare, and road networks.

International troops were used to help improve basic facilities to make life easier for families in Afghanistan. Many Afghans welcomed them, hopeful for the changes that their presence brought about, such as improved healthcare and educational opportunities for girls. However, supporting one side against the other often led to terrible family divisions.

In 2014, after most of the international troops had left Afghanistan, the U.N. recorded more than 3,500 civilian deaths and over 6,500 injuries in one year. This was more than in any year since the figures were recorded.

PUBLIC OPINION

In 2014, more than half of the people who responded to a survey carried out by the Asia Foundation said that they thought the country was heading in the right direction. In 2015, the figure dropped to just over one-third (36.7 percent) and 40 percent said they would leave the country if they had the opportunity.

Families were torn apart during the Afghanistan War, with many children orphaned or abandoned.

The ANA has lost thousands of men. Figures up until October 2015, show that Britain has lost 456 men and women. The United States has lost more than 2,000 men and women. Thousands suffered physical injuries and thousands more suffer from mental ill-health as a result of the horrific experience of the war.

Children born in Afghanistan in 2001 have only known fear into their teenage years. They have lived with bombings, shootings, and attacks on their communities. They have been treated with suspicion by international troops who may have suspected them as supporters and fighters. If they were known to sympathize with the Afghan or ISAF troops, they will have been targets for Taliban attacks.

LEARNING FROM WAR

Did the Soviets and then the Americans consider the history of Afghanistan and weigh the likelihood of a swift victory in the mountainous country? If they had, would they have gone to war in Afghanistan?

The United States began the war in response to a terrible terrorist attack on its people. The war has not resolved the situation in Afghanistan, although it has brought about some changes. People will look back at this period and ask whether or not the war could have been avoided. Would the Taliban have ruled Afghanistan if the Soviets had not invaded? People will also ask whether the war could have ended earlier, bringing a close to the cycle of death and destruction experienced in the war-torn country.

It is reported that Czar Babur (1483–1530), a founder of the Mughal dynasty that ruled much of central Asia in the sixteenth century, said,

> *"Afghanistan has not been and never will be conquered, and will never surrender to anyone."*

This may be true, but what kind of government will emerge in Afghanistan and will it offer respect and equality to its people?

The Afghanistan flag has often changed, reflecting the social and political upheaval the country has faced. The current flag features blocks of black, green, and red with the national emblem featuring a mosque in the center. Some people believe that the colors represent black for the dark periods of the country's history, red for the blood that has been lost during the battles for independence, and green for hope.

We can look back to try to find the reason a war started, but once we have understood the cause or causes, it is important to look to the future with a positive outlook and aim for peace and respect for all.

Can Afghanistan and the other countries caught up in its history move beyond the past and ongoing conflicts to establish a society free from fear and violence?

WEAVING HOPE

Afghan weavers are renowned for their rugs. These rugs often feature images that relate to war, such as tanks, helicopters, and guns. This reflects the many years that the Afghan people have been subjected to conflict. One day, perhaps the rug weavers can feature images of peace instead of war.

GLOSSARY

allies countries cooperating with each other for a common cause

aid money and equipment given to support another country

civilians people who are not in the army

civil war a war between two sides of the same country

communist the idea of having an equal society through government control of property and many other areas of life

democracy a system in which people can vote in elections to decide who will run their country

dominate to exert power

economic to do with the state of affairs of a country's finances

empires groups of countries controlled and run by one other country

ethnic from different religious or other backgrounds

justice to uphold the law in a fair way

madrassas educational institutions

military to do with the army

North Atlantic Treaty Organization (NATO) an international organization that brings together the armies of various countries, including Britain and the United States

political relating to the ideas and beliefs about society and communities, and the way a country is run

refugees people who have left their homes and often their countries to preserve their safety and well-being

Soviet Union a communist state from 1922 to 1991, made up of different countries, including Russia

terrorist a group or a person who tries to bring about change through acts of violence and terror

FOR MORE INFORMATION

BOOKS

Doeden, Matt and Blake Hoena. *War in Afghanistan: An Interactive Modern History Adventure* (You Choose: Modern History). North Mankato, MN: Capstone Press, 2014.

Steele, Philip. *Afghanistan: From War to Peace?* (Our World Divided). New York, NY: Rosen Central, 2012.

Zeiger, Jennifer. *The War in Afghanistan* (Cornerstones of Freedom). New York, NY: Scholastic, 2011.

WEBSITES

Find out more about Afghanistan, its people, country, customs, and history at:

www.afghan-web.com

Take a look at an interactive timeline of the history of war in Afghanistan at:

www.cfr.org/afghanistan/us-war-afghanistan/p20018

For regularly updated facts about Afghanistan visit:

www.cia.gov/library/publications/the-world-factbook/geos/af.html

For quick facts and figures, and information on the events leading up to the war, visit:

www.factmonster.com/country/afghanistan.html

INDEX